POMPEII

Robin Johnson

CRABTREE
Publishing Company
www.crabtreebooks.com

Crabtree Publishing Company

www.crabtreebooks.com

Author: Robin Johnson
Publishing plan research and development:
    Sean Charlebois, Reagan Miller
    Crabtree Publishing Company
Project coordinator: Kathy Middleton
Photo research: Robin Johnson, Sonya Newland
Editor: Sonya Newland
Proofreader: Crystal Sikkens
Design: Tim Mayer (Mayer Media)
Cover design: Margaret Amy Salter
Production coordinator and prepress
    technician: Ken Wright
Print coordinator: Katherine Berti

Produced for Crabtree Publishing
byWhite-Thomson Publishing

Reading levels determined by
Publishing Solutions Group.
Content level: R
Readability level: L

Photographs:
Alamy: National Geographic Image
    Collection: p. 15
Bridgeman Art Library: © Tabley House
    Collection, University of Manchester, UK:
    pp. 26–27
Corbis: p. 39; National Geographic Society:
    p. 14; Brooklyn Museum: p. 22; The Art
    Archive: pp. 24–25; Roger Ressmeyer:
    p. 45
Getty Images: The Bridgeman Art Library:
    pp. 1, 34–35; Gamma-Rapho: p. 8; French
    School: p. 9; De Agostini: pp. 10, 41, 42;
    DEA A. Dagli Orti: p. 13; Jean-Louis
    Desprez: p. 16; National Geographic:
    pp. 17, 20–21; John Millar Watt: p. 23; After
    Antonio Niccolini: pp. 30–31; C. L. Doughty:
    p. 31; Time & Life Pictures: p. 33
Mary Evans Picture Library: pp. 6–7, 12, 28–29,
    32, 36; Interfoto/ Sammlun Rauch: p. 18
Shutterstock: Sailorr: back cover, pp. 4–5, 44–45;
    kated: p. 38; Aaron Wood: p. 40
Wikipedia: pp. 42–43; Karl Briullov: front cover;
    Courtesy of Crew Creative Ltd: pp. 3, 19;
    Wolfgang Riga: p. 11

Library and Archives Canada Cataloguing in Publication

CIP available at Library and Archives Canada

Library of Congress Cataloging-in-Publication Data

Johnson, Robin (Robin R.)
Pompeii / Robin Johnson.
    pages cm. -- (Crabtree chrome)
Includes index.
ISBN 978-0-7787-7927-8 (reinforced library binding) -- ISBN
978-0-7787-7936-0 (paperback) -- ISBN 978-1-4271-7858-9
(electronic PDF) -- ISBN 978-1-4271-7973-9 (electronic HTML)
1. Pompeii (Extinct city)--Juvenile literature. 2. Vesuvius
(Italy)--Eruption, 79--Juvenile literature. I. Title.

DG70.P7J64 2013
937'.7256807--dc23

2012032204

Crabtree Publishing Company

www.crabtreebooks.com   1-800-387-7650

Printed in Canada/102012/MA20120817

Published in Canada	**Published in the United States**	**Published in the United Kingdom**	**Published in Australia**
Crabtree Publishing	Crabtree Publishing	Crabtree Publishing	Crabtree Publishing
616 Welland Ave.	PMB 59051	Maritime House	3 Charles Street
St. Catharines, ON	350 Fifth Avenue, 59th Floor	Basin Road North, Hove	Coburg North
L2M 5V6	New York, New York 10118	BN41 1WR	VIC 3058

Contents

Life in Pompeii

Mount Vesuvius

A volcano called Mount Vesuvius blew its top in 79 C.E. It blasted hot rock and ash high into the sky. The rock and ash fell on the nearby city of Pompeii for two days. Thousands of people died. The city was buried under thick layers of ash.

Lost and Found

Hundreds of years later, the lost city
of Pompeii was found. The ash had kept
Pompeii exactly as it had been so long ago.
Today, the **ruins** of Pompeii show us how
people lived and died in the ancient city.

▼ *Today, Mount
Vesuvius towers over
the ruins of Pompeii.*

A volcano is an opening in
the surface of Earth. When
volcanoes erupt, hot liquid
or solid rock and ash flow
from them. As the rock and
ash build up, some volcanoes
form tall mountains, such as
Mount Vesuvius.

ruins: parts of buildings that are left after a city has been destroyed

City by the Sea

Pompeii was a city that was part of the Roman **Empire**. It was close to Mount Vesuvius in southern Italy. Romans visited Pompeii for its warm, sunny weather. They built fine homes on the shore of the Bay of Naples.

◄ *Pompeii was a city near the Bay of Naples in southern Italy.*

▶ *Ships from Rome sailed to Pompeii, carrying goods.*

Danger Zone

The people of Pompeii lived and farmed very close to Mount Vesuvius. People did not know that the mountain was a deadly volcano. It had not erupted for hundreds of years. That was about to change.

Ancient Rome was the head of the Roman Empire. The city began around 750 B.C.E. Over time, Rome created a huge empire by taking over new lands and building large cities.

empire: a large area of land that is ruled by one leader or country

7

Booming City

In 79 C.E., the city of Pompeii was booming! It was a big, busy place. About 20,000 people lived there. Some people were very rich. Others were very poor. They all crowded into the shops, markets, **baths**, and narrow streets of Pompeii.

Food stand

Fountain

▲ *The poor people of Pompeii ate at food stands and got fresh water from public fountains.*

◄ *Hungry children hoped for scraps of food from the shops in Pompeii.*

Daily Life

The streets of Pompeii were full of life. People bought food at markets, bakeries, and food stands. Workers sold goods of all kinds in shops and from carts. Children played and dogs barked. People rushed through the noisy streets of the city.

There is a saying that "all roads lead to Rome." The Romans built thousands of long, straight roads. The roads joined the city of Rome to Pompeii and other places in the huge empire.

 baths: a public building with pools, for bathing and socializing

The Forum

The forum was a big open space in the middle of Pompeii. It was the heart of the city. People bought and sold goods in the forum. Friends met there. They watched parades and listened to speeches from their leaders.

Temple of Jupiter

Arch of Tiberius

Arch of Nero

▲ *Grand buildings like the Temple of Jupiter and arches in honor of Roman leaders stood in the forum in Pompeii.*

Roman Temples

People also went to temples in the forum and in other parts of the city. Temples were buildings that the Romans built for their gods. The people of Pompeii **worshiped** their gods at the temples and at home.

◄ *This picture of a god, a snake, and Mount Vesuvius was found in a home in Pompeii.*

Romans worshiped many gods. People believed the gods watched over them and controlled every part of their lives.

 worshiped: showing love and respect for gods

Comforts of Home

The wealthy people of Pompeii lived in big houses in the city. Some people also had **villas** in the country. The rich had many comforts. Their homes had heat and running water. They had lovely gardens and pools. They had fine art on their walls and floors.

▲ *The wealthy people of Pompeii lived in grand homes like this one.*

▲ *Actors performed plays and shows of all kinds in Pompeii theaters.*

Poor People

The poor people of Pompeii lived in crowded rooms in dirty buildings. They did not have heat, water, toilets, or other comforts. Poor people did not spend much time in their homes. They worked long hours in shops and on farms.

There was plenty to do in Pompeii! People watched plays in theaters. They cheered at fights and races held in large arenas.

 villas: large homes in the country

Vesuvius Erupts!

Strange Days

In the summer of 79 C.E., strange things began to happen in Pompeii. The water in the streams dried up. Mount Vesuvius began to rumble. The ground shook.

▲ *Men drank wine in taverns just before the volcano erupted. These were the last drinks the men would ever have.*

Warning Signs

On the morning of August 24, birds stopped singing. Dogs began to howl. The water in the bay got rough. Smoke began to pour out of Mount Vesuvius. The people of Pompeii did not know that these were signs of danger. They continued to work and play as usual.

▼ *A Roman soldier walking past a bakery in Pompeii is not worried by the smoke pouring out of the mountain behind him.*

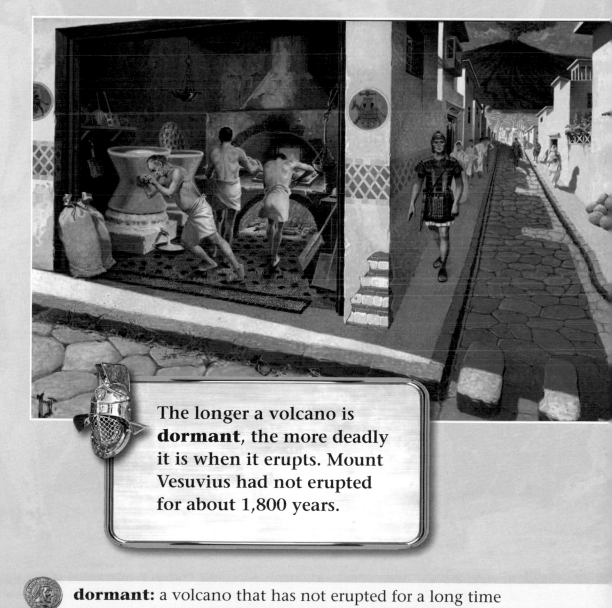

The longer a volcano is **dormant**, the more deadly it is when it erupts. Mount Vesuvius had not erupted for about 1,800 years.

dormant: a volcano that has not erupted for a long time

Blowing its Top

Suddenly, Mount Vesuvius erupted! There was a loud, fiery blast. The blast blew the top of the mountain right off. Mount Vesuvius began shooting hot rock and ash high into the sky.

▼ *As Mount Vesuvius erupted, it lit up the sky over Pompeii.*

On Shaky Ground

The blast from the volcano reached nearby Pompeii in seconds. The ground shook. Buildings trembled. All over the city, people screamed in surprise and fear. What was happening? Why was the sky on fire?

The **violent** blast surprised everyone in Pompeii. Some people were eating lunch. Others were hard at work. People rushed into the streets to see what was happening.

▲ *People in the streets were tossed into the air or thrown to the ground by the blast.*

 violent: very strong or powerful

17

Deadly Cloud

A huge black cloud began to form high over Mount Vesuvius. The cloud had an unusual size and shape. It looked like a tree with a large, flat top growing right out of the volcano.

Dangerous Drift

The cloud was filled with blazing hot ash and rock from the volcano. The wind began to blow the cloud toward Pompeii.

▲ *The deadly black cloud spread through the crowded streets of Pompeii.*

A man called Pliny the Younger saw Mount Vesuvius erupt from far away. He later wrote about the **disaster**. Pliny's letters help people today understand what happened on that day hundreds of years ago.

 disaster: a sudden accident that causes many deaths

Raining Ash

Hot ash began to rain down from the cloud. The ash landed on the terrified people below. Layers of white ash coated the streets and buildings of Pompeii. It looked like it was snowing in summer.

▼ *People covered their heads and ran for their lives as hot ash filled the streets of Pompeii.*

Gasping for Air

The thick ash choked the people of Pompeii. It filled their throats and lungs. They could not breathe. They could not even scream for help.

"Ashes were already falling, not as yet very thickly. I looked round: a **dense** black cloud was coming up behind us, spreading over the earth like a flood."

Pliny the Younger

dense: very thick

Falling Rocks

Rocks of all sizes began to fall
from the cloud. Some were
small **pumice** stones. Others
were huge rocks. These stones
and rocks rained down onto
the city streets and the
terrified people of Pompeii.

▲ *Rocks fell from the sky and smashed
into Pompeii's roads and buildings.*

Duck and Cover

Many people tried to dodge the rocks and escape to safety. Some people were hit by flaming rocks as they ran from the city. Others were trapped by large rocks that pinned them down or piled up around them.

> "As a protection against falling objects they put pillows on their heads tied down with cloths."
>
> Pliny the Younger

▼ *People rushed from arenas in panic, as flaming rocks fell all around them.*

pumice: light, glassy rock that forms in volcanoes

No Escape

Crashing Down

The earth shook. Ash and rocks kept falling on the city. The temples, baths, and other buildings in Pompeii swayed wildly. Some buildings crumbled and crashed to the ground.

Stay or Go?

The people of Pompeii had to decide quickly.
There was not a moment to lose. Should they
stay in the city? Or should they try to escape?
Pompeii was falling, but fires burned on the
roads leading out of the city. Nowhere was safe
for the people of Pompeii.

"They **debated** whether to stay
indoors or take their chance in
the open, for the buildings were
now shaking with violent
shocks, and seemed to be
swaying to and fro... Outside,
there was the danger of falling
pumice stones."

Pliny the Younger

◄ *Buildings tumbled down, crushing
the people inside them as well as
people on the streets outside.*

debated: thought about the good and bad points to decide what to do

Running for Their Lives

Most people tried to **flee** from the city. They grabbed what they could and ran for the hills. Some people carried bags of coins and other treasures. Other people had only the clothes on their backs.

▼ *Wild waves and thick ash kept the people of Pompeii from getting away by boat.*

Fleeing the Scene

Thousands of people all tried to flee at once. They pushed and shoved their way through the narrow streets. Some people fell and were crushed by the crowd. Others were killed by falling rocks as they ran away.

Some people tried to escape from Pompeii by boat, but they could not. The sea was filled with thick ash and rock. High waves crashed wildly against the shore.

flee: to run away from a place of danger

Taking Shelter

Some people thought it was safer to stay in Pompeii. They found **shelter** where they could. People crowded together in small, scared groups. They prayed to their gods. They hoped that the world was not ending.

▼ *People took shelter wherever they could, as far away as possible from the erupting volcano.*

Riches to Ruins

Some wealthy people stayed in Pompeii to protect their homes. The people did not want their nice things to be destroyed or stolen. Even the richest people in Pompeii could not save their homes or their own lives that day.

The people of Pompeii thought that angry gods had set the mountain and sky on fire. They begged the gods to save their families and homes. Their prayers were not answered.

shelter: a place that protects people from harm for a short time

29

Darkness Falls

Day to Night

By early evening, the big black cloud had moved higher in the sky. It blocked the Sun. Day looked like night. People were afraid of the sudden and total darkness.

Fires in the Dark

Sometimes bursts of flame lit up the sky. Fires broke out in the city. They were quickly put out by falling ash. Some people carried **torches** and lamps to light their way out of Pompeii. Others stumbled in the darkness.

▼ *Many people were crushed in the crowds as they tried to escape in the darkness.*

"You could hear the shrieks of women, the wailing of infants, and the shouting of men; some were calling their parents, others their children or their wives, trying to recognize them by their voices."

Pliny the Younger

torches: sticks of wood with flames on one end, used to light the way

No Way Out

It was very hard for people to leave Pompeii. They could not see in the dark. Thick piles of ash and rock filled the city and blocked the roads. Some people and animals were buried alive.

▲ *Thick layers of ash made it hard for people to escape from the city.*

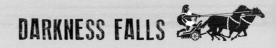

▲ *Some people were trapped beneath the heavy piles of rock and ash that filled the city.*

Nowhere to Hide

It was not safe to stay in Pompeii either. In some places, ash and rock reached the tops of the buildings! The ash and rock were heavy. The roofs of buildings **collapsed**. Ash burst through windows and choked the people inside.

"Ashes began to fall again, this time in heavy showers. We rose from time to time and shook them off, otherwise we should have been buried and crushed beneath their weight."

Pliny the Younger

 collapsed: fell or caved in suddenly

Deadly Waves

The next morning, things got worse. Deadly waves began to pour down Mount Vesuvius. The waves were made up of burning hot rock, ash, and **toxic** gas. They sped down the slopes of the volcano and into the city.

▶ *On the second day of the disaster, toxic gas and burning ash from the volcano killed anyone left in Pompeii.*

Burned and Buried

The hot rocks swept through Pompeii. The heat and gas killed any people or animals that were still alive. Thick layers of rock and ash buried the city. Only the tops of the tallest buildings could be seen.

The waves of hot gas and rock charged down the sides of the volcano. No one could outrun the fast and fiery waves or survive the extreme heat.

toxic: containing poison

The Smoke Clears

Mount Vesuvius erupted for two days. When it stopped, **survivors** tried to return home. People were shocked by what they saw. The great city of Pompeii was gone! It had vanished under a thick layer of ash.

▲ *Some people escaped from Pompeii before it was too late.*

Lost City

Nothing in Pompeii could be saved. The great forum, buildings, and roads were all buried. People left the city that was once so full of life. They started new lives in other parts of Italy. Over time, the world forgot about Pompeii.

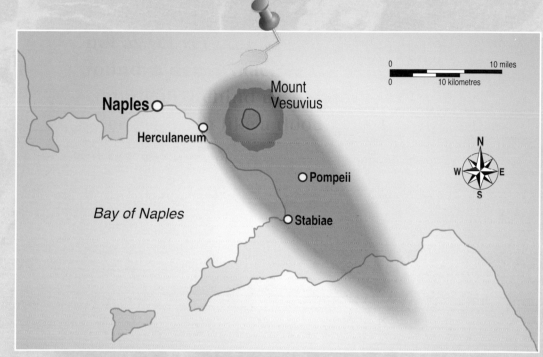

▲ The dark area on this map shows the places that were destroyed when Mount Vesuvius erupted.

Mount Vesuvius destroyed everything around it. Thousands of people died. All the animals and plants in the area were killed. Nearby towns were buried under thick layers of ash.

 survivors: people who stay alive when others have been killed

Frozen in Time

Lost and Found

Pompeii was lost for more than 1,600 years. In 1738, workers discovered a nearby town called Herculaneum. Like Pompeii, Herculaneum had been buried under ash when Mount Vesuvius erupted.

▲ *At Herculaneum, scientists uncovered large villas with wall paintings like this.*

▲ *Scientists discovered temples and other beautiful buildings buried under the ground in Pompeii.*

Buried Treasure

Ten years later, scientists began to **excavate** Pompeii. The scientists were amazed at what they found. The ash had kept the city of Pompeii exactly as it had been in 79 C.E. The ancient city had been frozen in time!

Scientists have been carefully excavating Pompeii for more than 250 years. They still have not finished digging out the great city.

 excavate: to dig out something from the ground

Slice of Life

The ruins of Pompeii show us what life was like long ago. They give us a look at how ancient Romans lived, worked, and played. The ruins show us the food that people ate. We can see the tools that people used and the art they made.

▲ *The ruins of Pompeii show us that Romans ate quick meals at food stands like this.*

Human Casts

The bodies of the people of Pompeii decayed. This left holes in the hard ash. Scientists poured **plaster** into these holes. They created casts of the people. From the casts, we can see what the people were doing when they died on that tragic day.

Scientists found all kinds of objects when they dug out Pompeii. They discovered coins on shop counters. They found dishes set at tables. They even found bread in an ancient oven!

▲ *Hot and cold foods were kept below the counters of food stands, so hungry people could eat quickly.*

 plaster: a material similar to cement that hardens when it dries

Learning from the Past

Scientists study the ruins of Pompeii to learn about the ancient Romans. Scientists have learned that Romans built huge villas, temples, theaters, and arenas. They built lovely homes and public baths. The Romans also built **aqueducts** to bring fresh water to cities.

▲ *The House of the Faun was a grand villa in Pompeii.*

Roman Life

Pompeii helps us understand many other things about life in the Roman Empire. We can see how the Romans invented new ways to build and grow their cities. We also know how Roman people kept clean and healthy.

▼ *Scientists found this faun statue in a home in Pompeii. A faun is a Roman forest god.*

"Rome wasn't built in a day."

It took the Romans many years to build Pompeii and the other cities in the empire. Now it will take scientists many years to fully discover the lost city of Pompeii.

aqueducts: long bridges used to bring water to places that need it

Pompeii Today

Millions of **tourists** visit Pompeii each year. People look at the crumbling walls that were once beautiful buildings. They walk down quiet streets that were once filled with noise and activity. The visiting tourists picture what life and death was like for the people of this ancient city.

▼ *Tourists from around the world explore the ancient ruins of Pompeii.*

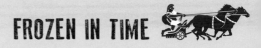

From the Grave

The ruins of Pompeii speak for the people who lived and died there. They tell the story of a powerful empire that changed the world. The ruins also tell the tale of a city that was buried alive one tragic day.

▼ *This cast from Pompeii shows a man covering his face to protect it from deadly ash.*

"From the end spring new beginnings."

Pliny the Elder, who died when Mount Vesuvius erupted

tourists: people who visit a place for fun

Learning More

Books

Life in Ancient Rome
by Shilpa Mehta-Jones
(Crabtree Publishing, 2005)

What the Romans Did for the World (Crabtree Connections)
by Alison Hawes
(Crabtree Publishing, 2011)

Graphic Library: Escape From Pompeii
by Terry Collins
(Capstone Press, 2010)

Pompeii: Lost and Found
by Mary Pope Osborne
(Alfred A. Knopf, 2006)

Through Time: Pompeii
by Richard Platt
(Kingfisher, 2007)

Movies

Pompeii: The Last Day
A non-fiction TV movie made
by the BBC in 2003

Websites

www.harcourtschool.com/ activity/pompeii/
Pompeii: Unraveling Ancient Mysteries

http://dsc.discovery.com/tv/ pompeii/
The Discovery Channel: Pompeii

http://rome.mrdonn.org/ pompeii.html
Ancient Rome for Kids: Pompeii

www.roman-empire.net/ children/index.html
Illustrated History of the Roman Empire: Children's Section

http://science.nationalgeographic .com/science/archaeology/pompeii/
National Geographic

Glossary

aqueducts Long bridges used to bring water to places that need it

baths a public building with pools, for bathing and socializing

collapsed Fell or caved in suddenly

debated Thought about the good and bad points to decide what to do

dense Very thick

disaster A sudden accident that causes many deaths

dormant A volcano that has not erupted for a long time

empire A large area of land that is ruled by one leader or country

excavate To dig out something from the ground

flee To run away from a place of danger

plaster a material similar to cement that hardens when it dries

pumice Light, glassy rock that forms in volcanoes

ruins Parts of buildings that are left after a city has been destroyed

shelter A place that protects people from harm for a short time

survivors People who stay alive when others have been killed

torches Sticks of wood with flames on one end, used to light the way

tourists People who visit a place for fun

toxic Containing poison

villas Large homes in the country

violent Very strong or powerful

worshiped Showing love and respect for gods

Index

Entries in **bold** refer to pictures